INTRICACIES
Poems of the heart

poems by

Joanna Kurowska

Finishing Line Press
Georgetown, Kentucky

INTRICACIES
Poems of the heart

ACKNOWLEDGMENTS

I gratefully acknowledge the following publications in which some of the
poems in this collection originally appeared:

Concise Delight: "The Poem," "Throwing Peas against The Wall"
Dziennik Związkowy (Chicago): Polish version of the poem "she and love"
Episteme: "Allotment"
*ken*again:* "Silence"
Levure littéraire: "Intricacies" (as "A Dream House")
Olentangy Review: "denial," "We"
Room Magazine: "The Woman With A Spider"

I am very grateful to Stefan Papp for letting me use the image of his oil canvas
Romeo and Juliet (1959) for my book's cover; to Paweł Młynarczyk for designing
the cover; to my husband John Brownell for his encouragement, patience, and
support.   /

Editor: Christen Kincaid

Cover Art: Stefan Papp

Author Photo: Paweł Młynarczyk

Cover Design: Paweł Młynarczyk

Printed in the USA on acid-free paper.
Order online: www.finishinglinepress.com
             also available on amazon.com

Author inquiries and mail orders:
Finishing Line Press
P. O. Box 1626
Georgetown, Kentucky 40324
U. S. A.

Table of Contents

I dedicate this painting to the memory of my friend Bohdan Kurowski.
Stefan Papp

Intricacies

There is a house, old and decrepit
I can take care of only in my sleep

Here is the living room—or a bathroom—
The water on the floor must be mopped

Here is the kitchen with a tree in its midst
Oh, so many spiders running up and down!

Here is a drawer full of yellowed letters
In a desk, near the wall soft with mold

Each time I venture to walk upstairs,
My feet plunge through the cracks

Whoever distributes sleep, please
make mine last longer

So that I can get smart with this house
before I wake up

Summer Day at the IU Campus

the red ant crosses the pavement
preoccupied with its purpose
to get out of the jungle of concrete
and return to the ant-heap business

the chipmunks sport on the grass
escaping from under my feet
they playfully dramatize the threat
that the two-legged monster brings

the wind plays with the clouds
soon the sun gets involved
for a moment, the passing man
stops pondering his own importance

he mutters: It looks like rain

* * *

he is opening his mouth
I don't know what will fly out of it
a pink-feathered bird
a death's head moth or
an insect with a sharp sting

Allotment

Enough! Come out of those yellow eyes of fear!
The greedy day grabs you and me by the hands.
Have you been wronged, with your rosary of tears?
Look, our dreams hit the wall in equal shares.

Here's a tree and rain. How can we divide them?
On my way home today, I've got soaking wet.
Do you think I could trade the rain for a tree,
when it's pouring outside and the trees stand bare?

Don't fall asleep so quickly—the night is young.
Twigs of sadness clank at my window and yours.
The morning divides the world into two halves…
a thread of air binds us; we need nothing more.

The Poem

you refuse to understand my smile
the poem is so much stronger than I
it can freely talk about desire
passionless, it will keep talking after I die

A Cut

dying of thirst,
the mailbox
has bitten me
with its stingy splinter

the makeup

i love your makeup, he said; she made haste
to the matter's other side—like a spring breeze

she had flown away—to that he was blind—
carelessly, she left her makeup behind

the face-contour still hovered in the air
the cheeks' blush, lips' curve, eyelashes' hair

so much did he love that facial idea
oblivious to its void, he took it for real

he kissed the lipstick with passion intense
the cheeks' dry rouge became all dense

he found the face powder simply enchanting
caressing it with his lips he went on panting

the eyelashes quivered, half-closed with delight
the eye-shadow darkened, befitting the night

so did they remain, he on his love centered
the matter two-sided, her makeup perfect

The Woman with a Spider

no one has ever loved the black spider
so the woman loved it

she speaks to it caressingly
feeds it with sweet milk

it walks about her apartment
its hairy legs astride

she combs its hair
with a tiny soft brush

its legs shiver, hard to say
if out of pleasure or rage

when she touches it
it plunges its teeth in her flesh

and secretes deadly venom
in miniscule doses

not out of avarice but from cunning
for if it killed the woman

who would comb its hair
with a tiny soft brush

she and love

every night
when the whole house is asleep
they fight with each other

she—holding a knife
love—holding a poison

every morning
greets them changed
her—more and more sick
love—more and more hurt

On Parting

Some book hasn't been read
a gun fired or a flower laid
Something uncertain, a word or glance
is trying to take shape in wistful silence

meaning

on the shelf, a couple of empty bottles
the golden wine drunk throughout the night
it was the new year's eve. We were divine
did time happen before or after we touched?

outside the door, God waited tenaciously
eager to pour meaning into our glasses
as soon as they were unfilled

now I pour oil from one bottle into the other
and use a match to ignite the flame
I place a tiny brass cross beneath the couple,
trying to understand

At night

At night the world lies in my bed
its voracious mouth open wide
I cannot see the edges of its lips
Every night I fall into it

denial

with my elbow, I draw
your breath in
the sand

my skin's tips still
sensing the hue
of your echo

the toes licking
your voice's
scent

the nostrils flared,
I hear your eyes'
gray-blue;

drowning the thought
of what you
have done

Rolling on Skates

I'm still permitted
to pin on to your shoulders
the absent angels
too busy to descend
or obedient to the One
who allows failure

you resemble a little boy
when, completely drunk
in an unbuttoned shirt,
wind blowing into your hair,
you roll on children's skates
into the arms of death

An Embrace

The extended arms do not know limits
trying to embrace the forest's fragrance
the skin's luster and the sunset's hue

But when one hand meets the other
The arms' wedding ring tightens
around parched hunger

* * *

But what will happen to our talk stopped in a scream
Your eyes tightly filling the aquarium of silence
I thought scream was an arrow aiming at heaven
But it too drifts on calm waters to the land of shadows

Reading

I don't even notice this non-love in me
in this strain of thought, the eternal talk
you are sick, but I don't hear or see
I only know. It's eleven o'clock

someone else

love happens to someone else
marriage happens to someone else
childbirth happens to someone else
parting happens to someone else
illness happens to someone else
death happens to someone else

what is happening to me?

Silence

this sudden silence
comes like a stranger
bereft of the tongue's impatience
the lips' excursions
the fingers' cleverness
the skin's warm pools

after all the I-love-you-s
and you-look-great-s
at first it seems oppressive
my breath withheld
slowly, I begin to discern
silence's love-message

Throwing Peas against the Wall

You want to hurt me.
I know it by the set of your mouth
and your angry gaze.
Sentence-pods explode with a blast,
hard balls of words
hit me in the face.

I stare at them, amazed,
thinking: Dear God, it's spring.

Now

I am awakening from a future,
I am returning from a past

Birds are singing, the grass is green
the wind is caressing my cheeks

Winds do not blow in the future;
Birds do not sing in the past

No longer waiting for salvation,
I'm letting go bygone sins

To the English Language

You said "I love you"
and "I can't love you"
and "I don't love you any more"

You raised my hopes
breathed ecstasy into my neck
spelled out rejection

Having known you—my maker
I sat down and wrote a poem
Now, look: I have made you

Untitled

I asked for signs but
all I could get was
the ordinary world

the wind, the sky, news
good and bad, music
behind the wall

Backward Train

I don't want this man
staring at me from the
opposite row, to know
I've missed my stop.

Getting onto the platform,
I hide behind a pole
until his face in the window
vanishes from my sight.

Then, only then, I hop
onto my backward train.

The Door

In the morning, I touch my ear
to the door. I hear its heartbeat.

Its one face turned towards me,
the other looking at the world.

Behind it, a day unfolds. I can
feel its pulse with my fingertips.

I put my hand on the knob.
The door trembles, will I open it?

We

For John

One night I woke up to your face:
a white patch sewn upon darkness.
The night's black hole was repaired.
I gazed into your eyes' pools.

It was as if we were in the silence
of a deep, deep ocean—two fish
sending messages indiscernible
to any ear. Our bodies talked.

What priests and rulers fear
is always beyond their reach,
was happening. The Universe's
golden vein—life—branched out.

Life happened. Smiling, we were
set free. As usual, faithful death
sat near us. We did not know yet
she was a friend—we do now.

Yes, there are those who kill,
who put people in cattle cars,
those, who never have enough;
whose homes are balloons of fear.

We went out and saw myriads of stars
burning and falling, and being born
in silence. Among them, you and I
patching light onto the night's dome.

Joanna Kurowska is the author of six critically acclaimed poetry collections, *Stained Glass* (eLectio Publishing, 2016); *The Butterfly's Choice* (Broadstone Books, 2015); *Inclusions* (Cervena Barva Press, 2014); *The Wall & Beyond* (eLectio Publishing, 2013); Obok : Near (Oficyna Literacka, 1999, Poland); and *Ściana : The Wall* (Wydawnictwo Dolnośląskie, 1997, Poland).

Kurowska's poems, flash fiction, and scholarly work have been published widely in American and European journals, such as *Acolada* (Romania), *Atticus Review, Bateau, The Conradian* (UK), *Episteme* (India), *Fraza* (Poland), *International Poetry Review, Journal of Religion and The Arts, Kultura* (Paris), *Levure littéraire, Room Magazine* (Canada), *Slavic & East European Journal, Southern Quarterly*, and elsewhere.

Kurowska has taught for many years at Indiana University, Bloomington, and the University of Chicago. She currently works as an independent scholar and writer.